Festivals through the Year
Summer

Anita Ganeri

Heinemann
LIBRARY

First published in Great Britain by Heinemann Library
Halley Court, Jordan Hill, Oxford OX2 8EJ
a division of Reed Educational and Professional Publishing Ltd.
Heinemann is a registered trademark of Reed Educational & Professional Publishing Limited.

OXFORD MELBOURNE AUCKLAND IBADAN JOHANNESBURG
BLANTYRE GABORONE PORTSMOUTH (NH) USA CHICAGO

Designed by Ken Vail Graphic Design, Cambridge
Illustrations by Pat Murray
Printed by Wing King Tong in Hong Kong

02 01 00 99
10 9 8 7 6 5 4 3 2

ISBN 0 431 05457 6

British Library Cataloguing in Publication Data

Ganeri, Anita
Summer. – (Festivals through the year)
1. Summer festivals – Great Britain – Juvenile literature
I. Title
394.2'63'0941

Acknowledgements
The Publishers would like to thank the following for permission to reproduce photographs:
BBC/David Noton, p. 4; Celtic Picture Library, pp. 22, 23; Circa Photo Library (John Fryer) p. 11,
(B.J. Mistry) p. 24; Collections, (Davis, Richard) p. 17, (Tordai, John), p. 28, (Watts, Paul) p.14;
Greenhill, Sally, pp. 6, 7; Harjinden Singh Sagoo, pp. 12, 13; Robert Harding Picture Library, p. 20;
Soester, Juliette, pp. 8, 9; The Stock Market, p. 19; Tony Stone Images (Brooke, Marcus) p. 27,
(Giles, Roy) p. 26.

Cover photograph reproduced with permission of Collections/John Tordai

Our thanks to Peter Woodward, who works with SHAP Working Party on World
Religions in Education, for his comments in the preparation of this book.

Every effort has been made to contact copyright holders of any material reproduced in this book.
Any omissions will be rectified in subsequent printings if notice is given to the Publisher.

Contents

Words printed in **bold letters like these** are explained in the Glossary.

Celebrating summer

Most people are glad when summer comes. It is the time for being out of doors, with warm days and long, lazy evenings. It is the perfect time for holidays. Summertime gardens are filled with flowers, and farmers' fields are filled with ripening crops.

Many festivals are held in summertime. Many take place out of doors. Some celebrate the warmth and light of the Sun. Others have special religious meanings, when people remember the lives of their gods or teachers and important times in their religion's history.

In summer, nature is in full bloom, with flowers and new plants growing in the hedgerows.

Festivals are often happy times with many ways of celebrating. There are special services and ceremonies, delicious food, dancing, cards and gifts. Some festivals are holidays when you have a day off school.

Some festivals happen on the same day each year. Others change from year to year. For festivals that change, you will find a dates circle, which tells you when the festival will be. (The future dates of some festivals are only decided upon nearer the time, so some dates in the circles may be out by a day or two.)

Dates

7 August 1998
26 August 1999
15 August 2000
4 August 2001
6 August 2002

Moon dates

The calendar we use every day has a year of 365 days, divided into 12 months. Most months have 30 or 31 days. Some religions use different calendars which are based on the Moon. A Moon month is the time it takes for the Moon to travel around the Earth. This is about 27 days, which gives a shorter year. So, each year, the Moon calendar falls out of step with the everyday calendar. This is why some festivals fall on different days each year.

May Day

The first of May is May Day. It used to mark the first day of summer when the first **hawthorn** (May) blossoms were seen. A great festival was held to celebrate. Some old **customs** continue today.

In some places, people dance around a Maypole. The Maypole is made from a tree trunk, decorated with long, colourful ribbons. Each dancer holds a ribbon and skips around the pole so the ribbons become twisted together. Then they dance the other way so the ribbons begin to unwind.

Dancing around a maypole.

Another May Day dance is done by Morris dancers. As they dance, they shake rattles and bells, stamp their feet and bang two sticks together. This is meant to scare away evil winter spirits and bring a good summer.

Morris dancers help to make sure that the summer will be a good one.

The nearest Monday to May Day is a holiday. This holiday began about 100 years ago for factory workers. They worked very long hours and May Day was a welcome day off.

Bonfires and dew

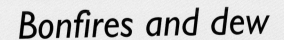

The ancient name for the May Day festival was Beltane. On this day, people got up early to wash in the morning **dew**. This was said to bring beauty and good health. They also lit great bonfires for good luck.

Shavuot

The **Jewish** festival of Shavuot happens in May or June. At this time, **Jews** remember how, long ago, God gave the Ten **Commandments** to **Moses**.

Dates
31 May 1998
21 May 1999
9 June 2000
28 May 2001
17 May 2002

At Shavuot, synagogues are decorated with flowers and fruit.

At Shavuot in the **synagogue**, there is a service when the story of Moses is read from the Torah, the Jews' **holy** book. After the service, people eat a special meal. For this, loaves of bread are baked with ladder shapes on top.

These loaves remind people that Moses had to climb a mountain (Mount Sinai) to talk to God. For the two days of the festival, Jewish children do not have to go to school.

Ladder bread is baked especially for Shavuot.

The Ten Commandments

These are ten rules which tell people how they should live.

1 I am the Lord your God. You must not worship any other gods but me.
2 Do not make any idols (statues) to worship.
3 Do not use God's name in a bad way.
4 Keep the **Shabbat** day (Saturday) holy.
5 Respect your father and mother.
6 Do not kill.
7 Do not have affairs.
8 Do not steal.
9 Do not tell lies about others.
10 Do not be jealous of others.

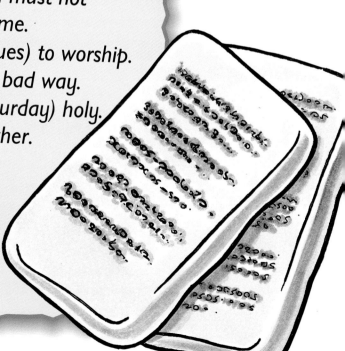

Pentecost

Fifty days after **Easter**, **Christians** celebrate the festival of Pentecost. They remember how the first Christians were given the gift of the **Holy Spirit**.

This meant that they were filled with God's power. They could now do the things **Jesus** did, such as teaching people about God and making ill people well again. From then on, they began to spread **Christianity** all over the world. This is why some people call Pentecost the birthday of Christianity.

The white dove represents the Holy Spirit.

White Sunday

Another name for Pentecost is Whit Sunday or Whitsuntide. This used to be a favourite day for people to be **baptized**. This means joining the Christian Church. The day was called White (Whit) Sunday because they wore white clothes.

At Pentecost, many Christians join in special walks called processions. Some carry a **banner** with the name of their **church** sewn onto it. This is a way of showing that they are proud of their beliefs. There are also special services in church.

Dates

31 May 1998
23 May 1999
11 June 2000
3 June 2001
19 May 2002

A procession for Pentecost.

Guru Arjan's Death

On 16 June every year, **Sikhs** remember the death of **Guru Arjan**, one of their greatest teachers. Guru Arjan lived almost 300 years ago in India. The **emperor** wanted him to give up his religion. But Guru Arjan refused and so he was killed.

To mark this time, Sikhs hold a special festival called a **Gurpurb**. The Guru Granth Sahib, the Sikhs' **holy** book, is read out in the **Gurdwara**. This takes about two whole days and nights. Readers take it in turns to read for up to two hours at a time.

Reading the Guru Granth Sahib in the Gurdwara is an important part of a Gurpurb festival.

Making karah parshad

At Sikh services and festivals, people share a sweet food called karah parshad. Sharing shows that God sees them as equals.

Sharing out karah parshad.

Try making your own karah parshad. Ask an adult to help you.

You will need:
200 g each of butter, sugar and semolina
half a cup of water

What to do:
1 Melt the butter in a pan.
2 Add the semolina and cook until golden brown, stirring all the time.
3 Mix in the sugar and water.
4 Cook gently until the mixture thickens.
5 Leave to cool, then serve.

Dragon Boat Festival

More than 2000 years ago in China there was a famous poet called Ch'u Yuan. He did not like the cruel way in which the **emperor** treated ordinary people. But the emperor would not listen to him. In despair, Ch'u Yuan threw himself into a river. At once, the local people took out their dragon boats and rushed to save him. But they could not reach him in time.

Dragon boat racing in Falmouth, Cornwall.

Every year, in May or June, Chinese people mark Ch'u Yuan's death with a festival. The highlight of the day are the dragon boat races. They are held to remember the race to save Ch'u Yuan's life. The boats are long, slim rowing boats, brightly painted to look like dragons, with a dragon's head at one end. Someone beats a drum to keep the rowers in time. Everyone wants their boat to win.

Dates

30 May 1998
18 June 1999
6 June 2000
25 June 2001
15 June 2002

Special dumplings

After the racing, there is a feast. People eat rice **dumplings**, wrapped in bamboo leaves. They are filled with meat, nuts, fruit and egg. Legend says that local people threw dumplings like these into the river to stop the fish eating Ch'u Yuan's body.

Midsummer's Day

Midsummer's Day is on 21 June. This is the longest day of the year, when the Sun is at its strongest. Long ago, people worshipped the Sun as a god. At Midsummer, they celebrated the Sun's power with bonfires and torchlit parades. People danced around the bonfires like the Sun dancing across the sky. There was also a great feast.

These celebrations were a way of asking the Sun to keep on shining brightly. People knew that, after Midsummer, the days would get shorter and the nights longer. They did not want summer to end.

Summer flowers

People worshipped the Sun because the Sun gave them warmth and light, and helped their crops to grow. At Midsummer, they decorated their houses with bunches of wild flowers. Bright blue cornflowers were hung on the front door.

Druids worshipping the Sun at Stonehenge.

Today, very few people celebrate Midsummer's Day. In the past a great ceremony was held at **Stonehenge** in Wiltshire. Here **priests**, called **Druids**, worshipped the Sun. Some people still meet at Stonehenge to watch the Sun rise on Midsummer's Day.

Milad al-Nabi

At Milad al-Nabi, **Muslims** celebrate the birthday of the **Prophet Muhammad (pbuh)**. He was born in the city of **Makkah** in Saudi Arabia long ago. Muhammad is very important for Muslims. They believe that **Allah** sent messages to Muhammad. These were collected together as the Qur'an, the Muslims' **holy** book. Muhammad spent the rest of his life teaching people to follow Allah.

To mark this important day, Muslims go to the **mosque** to hear readings from the Qur'an and stories about Muhammad's life. It is a good time for children to learn about Muhammad. Muslims also remember Muhammad's death on the same day.

Showing respect

When Muslims talk about Muhammad, they always add the words 'peace be upon him' after his name to show respect. This is often written as pbuh.

St Swithin's Day

Watch out for the weather on 15 July! This is St Swithin's Day. The saying goes that if it rains on St Swithin's Day, it will rain for the next 40 nights and days. If it is dry, the weather will stay fine.

Legend says that St Swithin was the **Bishop** of Winchester, in Hampshire, more than 1000 years ago. Before he died, he asked to be buried outside in the churchyard like an ordinary person. This was done. But the **monks** wanted to move him to a grander tomb inside the **cathedral**. To show how cross he was, he made it rain for 40 days and nights. So the monks changed their minds and left him in peace.

Rain clouds on St Swithin's Day.

Asala

At the Asala festival in July, **Buddhists** remember the **Buddha**'s first **sermon**. The Buddha spent many years trying to discover why people's lives are unhappy and how to make them better. One day, he saw things clearly. He understood the truth about life. In his first sermon, he taught his followers a better way to live. This was called the Noble Eight-fold Path.

Candles on a Buddhist shrine.

During the festival, Buddhists visit the **vihara** to hear the **monks** give talks about the Buddha. They also bring gifts of food and candles. The candles have a special meaning. Buddhists believe that the Buddha's teachings help people to understand life better, just as the candle-light helps them to see better.

Dates

19 July 1998
28 July 1999
16 July 2000
5 July 2001
Later dates not known

The wheel

A wheel with eight spokes is a very important Buddhist sign. Each spoke stands for one step on the Noble Eight-fold Path.

1 Right understanding – of the Buddha's teachings.
2 Right thought – thinking good, kind thoughts.
3 Right speech – not telling lies.
4 Right action – not killing or stealing. Being kind to others.
5 Right work – doing a job that does not hurt others.
6 Right effort – working hard to do good.
7 Right mindfulness – thinking before you act or speak.
8 Right concentration – training your mind to be peaceful.

Eisteddfod

In the first week of August, Welsh people hold a special festival of music, poetry, singing and dancing. This is called the National **Eisteddfod**. There are competitions to find the best writers and performers. Most important of all is the poetry competition. Poems are written many weeks beforehand. Then the winner's name is announced at the Eisteddfod. The first prize is a beautiful silver crown. It is a very great honour to win.

The writer of the winning poem sits on a throne and wears a silver crown.

At the Eisteddfod, people show how proud they are to be Welsh. They wear their traditional costumes and speak in the Welsh language. All the competitions are also in Welsh.

There are lots of smaller eisteddfods during the summer. One of them is just for children. There is also an International Music Eisteddfod for people from all over the world.

Dressing up for Eisteddfod.

Write a poem

Try writing your own poem about summer. Keep it short, about six to eight lines. You can write it in English if you do not know Welsh! Do you think it would win the silver crown?

Raksha Bandhan

The **Hindu** festival of Raksha Bandhan happens in August. On this day, a girl ties a colourful bracelet around her brother's right wrist to protect him from evil. The bracelet is called a **rakhi**. In return, her brother promises to look after her in the coming year. The brother also gives his sister some money as a present. In Hindu families, cousins and sometimes friends can join in, too.

A rakhi is made of twisted thread or ribbon, decorated with beads and gold threads. In India, you can buy rakhis from market stalls, like this one.

There are many stories explaining how the festival began. One tells of a war between the gods and the demons. The wife of the god Indra tied a rakhi around his wrist to keep him safe.

Dates

7 August 1998
26 August 1999
15 August 2000
4 August 2001
Later dates not known

Another story tells of a warrior whose grandmother gave him a rakhi. While he wore the rakhi, he came to no harm. But when his rakhi broke, he was killed in battle.

Raksha means 'protection'.
Bandhan means 'tie'.

Making a rakhi

Try making your own rakhi from a piece of card, stuck on to a piece of ribbon or thread.

Decorate the card with glitter, sequins, tinsel or tiny beads. You can stick these on with glue.

Highland Games

In August and early September, Highland Games take place all over Scotland. They began hundreds of years ago when the **chiefs** of the **clans** called people together to take part in contests of strength and skill. Then the chiefs picked the winners for their armies.

Going to the Games is great fun. There are tests of strength, such as throwing the hammer and tossing the caber. A caber is a large, heavy log which competitors throw as far as they can. If the caber is too heavy for anyone to toss it, more and more of the log is cut off until it can be thrown.

Tossing the caber is very hard work!

26

Scottish dancing.

Other events test people's speed and fitness. These include running events, such as the hill race. Runners have to race to the top of the nearest hill, then race back down again. Then there are piping contests, Scottish dancing, wrestling and a tug-of-war. There are also pillow fights and everyone joins in!

Playing the bagpipes

*You can tell what **bagpipes** look like from their name. They are like a large bag or pouch, with several pipes sticking out. You blow down the pipes to puff the bag out and make different sounds. It takes a lot of practice!*

27

Notting Hill Carnival

Every summer, a huge open-air party is held in Notting Hill in London. The end of August is carnival time. A carnival is a special parade. The streets are filled with beautifully decorated floats and dancers dressed in fabulous costumes. People spend many months getting everything ready. Steel bands play lively music to listen and dance to, and there are lots of delicious things to eat. Thousands of people go to watch and take part.

Dancers at the Notting Hill Carnival wear colourful costumes.

The first Notting Hill Carnival happened in 1961. It was started by people who came from the **West Indies** to live in London. In the West Indies, people held their carnival in January or February. But in Britain, this was the coldest time of year. So they moved the carnival to summertime instead.

Carnival masks

Make a spectacular carnival mask from card. Perhaps you could cut the mask into a Sun shape for summer. Cut out two holes for your eyes. Then paint it or decorate it with shiny paper, and maybe sequins and feathers, too. Tape a stick to one side of your mask so you can hold it in front of your face.

Glossary

Allah – Muslim word for God

bagpipes – musical instrument often played in Scotland

banner – large flag

baptized – when a person is baptized, they become a full member of the Christian Church at a special service

bishop – very senior Christian priest

Buddha – great teacher who lived about 2500 years ago

Buddhist – person who follows the teachings of the Buddha

cathedral – important Christian church, where a bishop (senior priest) is based

chief – leader or ruler

Christianity – religion of the Christians

Christian – person who follows the teachings of Jesus

church – Christian place of worship

clan – Scottish family group

Commandments – holy laws or rules

custom – special way of doing things, such as celebrating a festival

dew – small drops of water you see on flowers or grass early in the morning

Druid – sort of priest who worshipped the Sun long ago

dumpling – small parcel of food wrapped in pastry

Easter – spring festival at which Christians remember how Jesus died and how he came back to life again

eisteddfod – Welsh festival of singing, dancing and poetry

emperor – ruler of a country, like a king

Gurdwara – Sikh place of worship

Gurpurb – Sikh festival which celebrates the birth or death of one of the Gurus (Sikh teachers)

Guru Arjan – Sikh leader who was killed for his beliefs. The word Guru means teacher.

hawthorn – bushy tree or shrub which flowers in summer. Its flowers are also called May blossom.

Hindu – to do with the Hindu religion, which began in India about 4500 years ago. A Hindu is someone who follows the Hindu religion.

holy – means respected because it is to do with God

Holy Spirit – Christian name for God's power in the world

Jesus – religious teacher who lived about 2000 years ago. Christians believe that he was the son of God.

Jewish – to do with the Jewish religion

Jew – person who follows the Jewish religion, which began in the Middle East more than 4000 years ago

Makkah – city in the country we now call Saudi Arabia where the Prophet Muhammad pbuh was born. It is the Muslims' holiest place.

monk – man who gives up his possessions and devotes his life to God. Buddhist monks devote their lives to the Buddha. Monks have to obey a strict set of rules.

Moses – great Jewish leader who lived about 3500 years ago

mosque – Muslim place of worship

Muhammad – last great prophet of Islam. He was chosen by Allah to teach people how to live.

Muslim – person who follows the religion of Islam

pbuh – these letters stand for 'peace be upon him'. Muslims add these words after Muhammad's name and the names of the other prophets.

priest – holy man or religious leader

prophet – person chosen by God to be his messenger

rakhi – bracelet tied by a sister around a brother's wrist during the Hindu festival of Raksha Bandhan

sermon – a talk

Shabbat – Jewish holy day. It lasts from sunset on Friday to sunset on Saturday. No work is allowed on the Shabbat.

Sikh – person who follows the Sikh religion, which began in India about 500 years ago

Stonehenge – great circle of stones in Wiltshire, England. It may have been an ancient temple for worshipping the Sun.

synagogue – Jewish place of worship

vihara – Buddhist monastery or place of worship

West Indies – group of islands in the Caribbean Sea

Index